Cut It Out!

Cool Paper Projects for Creative Kids

Written and illustrated by Brian White

ISBN: 9781086880434

PROJECTS

Grumpy Nesting Gnomes

Madcap Monster Maker

Door Hanger

Soup Can Prank

Pet Bugs

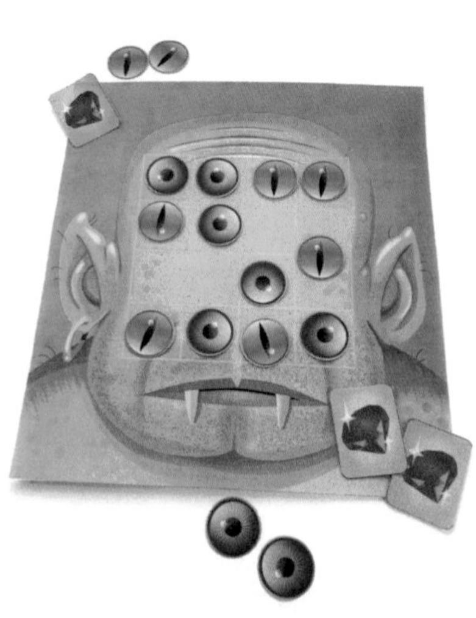

Ogre-Slayer Game

PROJECTS

Paper Crystals

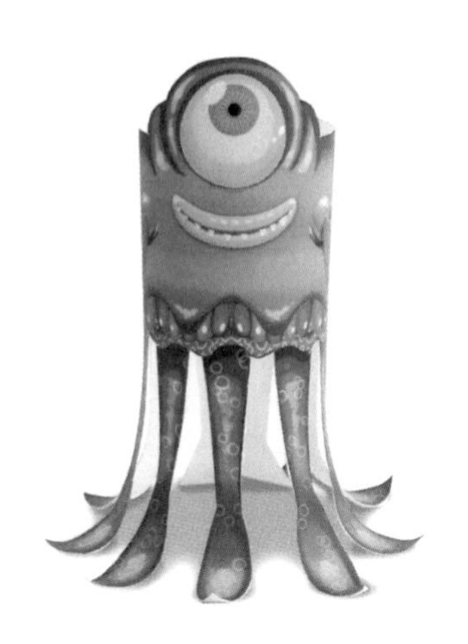

Sea Creature

Borrowed Bookmarks

Clone Match Game

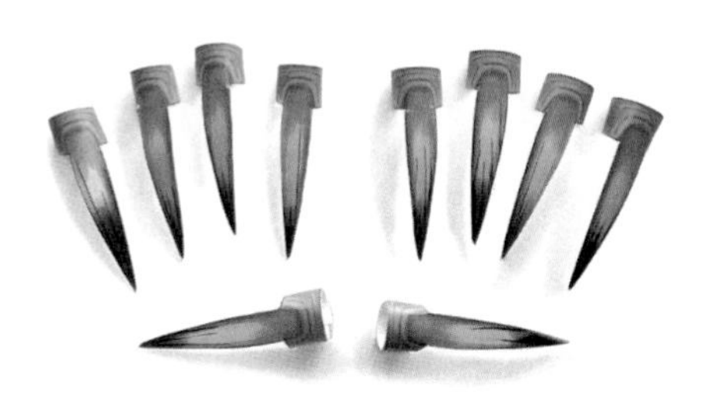

Creepy Claws

Misfortune Teller

Things you will need:

Scissors

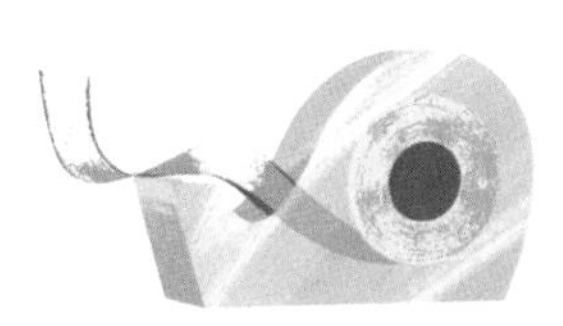

Tape

Glue and toothpicks

(Squirt some glue onto a paper plate and apply with toothpicks)

Pencil

Hints and Tips:

Carefully remove the entire page from the book before you start making a project

Go slow! Take your time cutting and gluing

Types of folds:

Mountain Fold

(the fold points up)

Valley Fold

(the fold points down)

Borrowed Bookmarks

Slip one of these hilarious bookmarks inside the pages of your favorite book when you loan it to a friend.

1. Carefully cut out along the solid lines
2. Write your name inside the white rectangle.

cut the page from the book before you start making this project

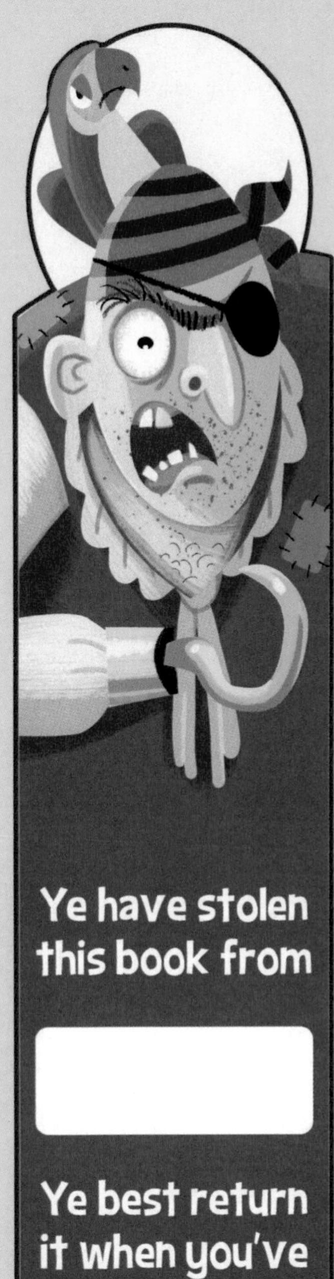

Creepy Claws

Slip these frightening fingernails onto your fingertips to scare your friends and family.

1. Carefully cut out along the solid outlines.
2. Place one claw over your fingernail and wrap the tabs behind so they fit your fingertips snugly.
3. Tape the loop to fit.
4. Repeat with all fingers.

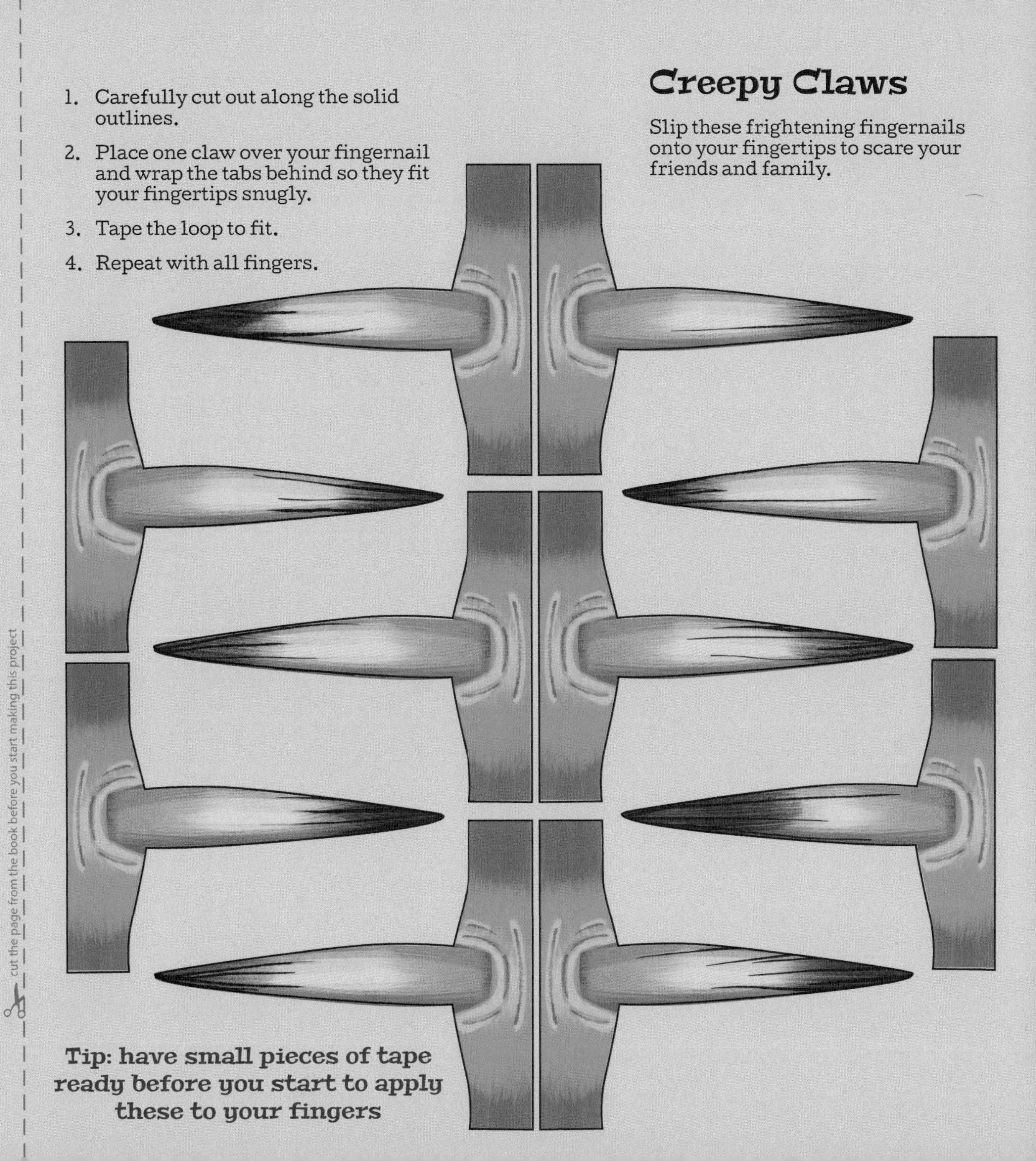

Tip: have small pieces of tape ready before you start to apply these to your fingers

cut the page from the book before you start making this project

Sea Creature

Make this wacky Sea Creature to decorate your desk or bedside table.

1. Carefully cut out along the solid lines.
2. Roll it into a tube and secure with glue or tape.
3. Curl the bottom of the legs outward by wrapping them around a pencil so the creature will stand on its own.

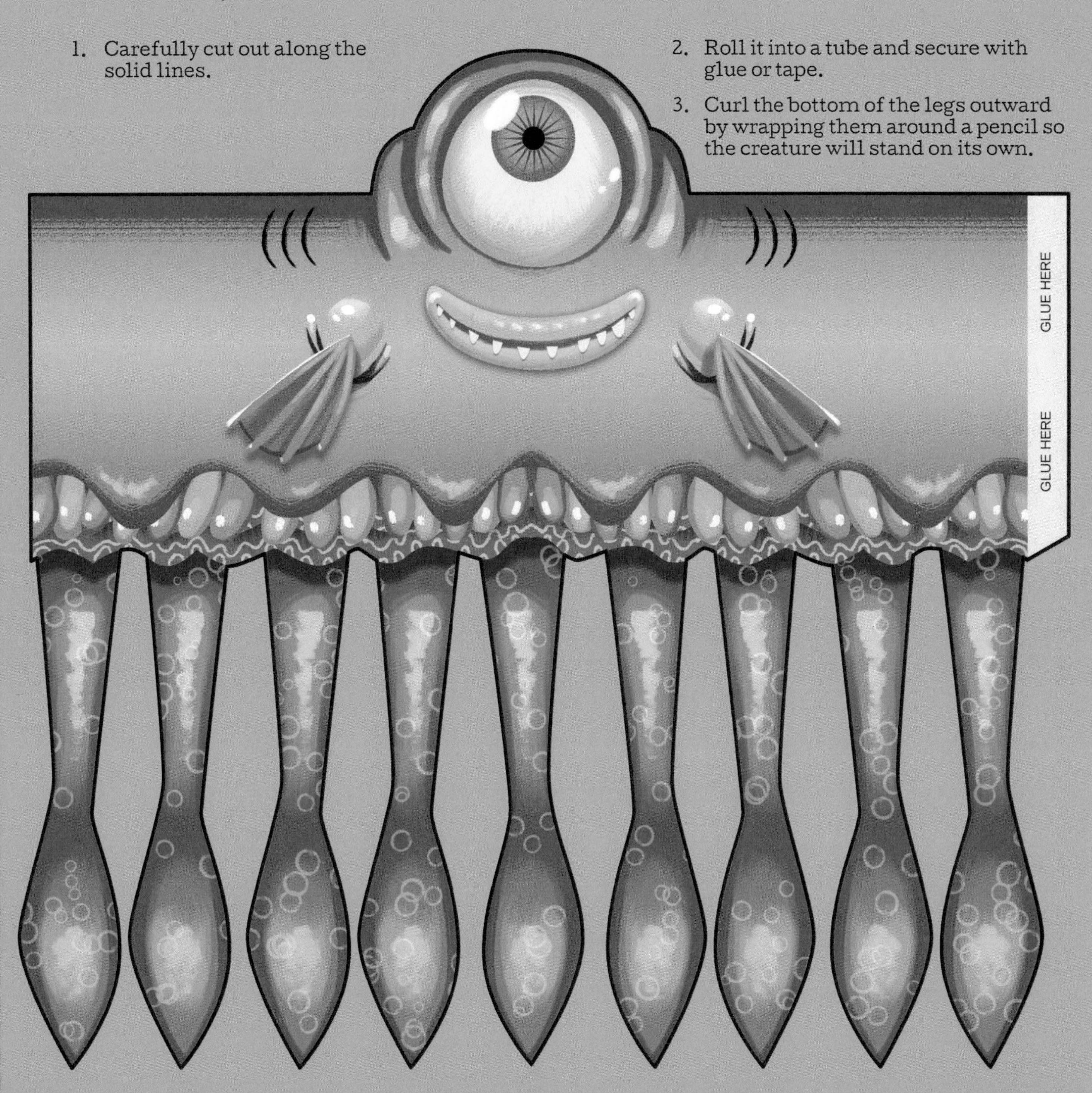

cut the page from the book before you start making this project

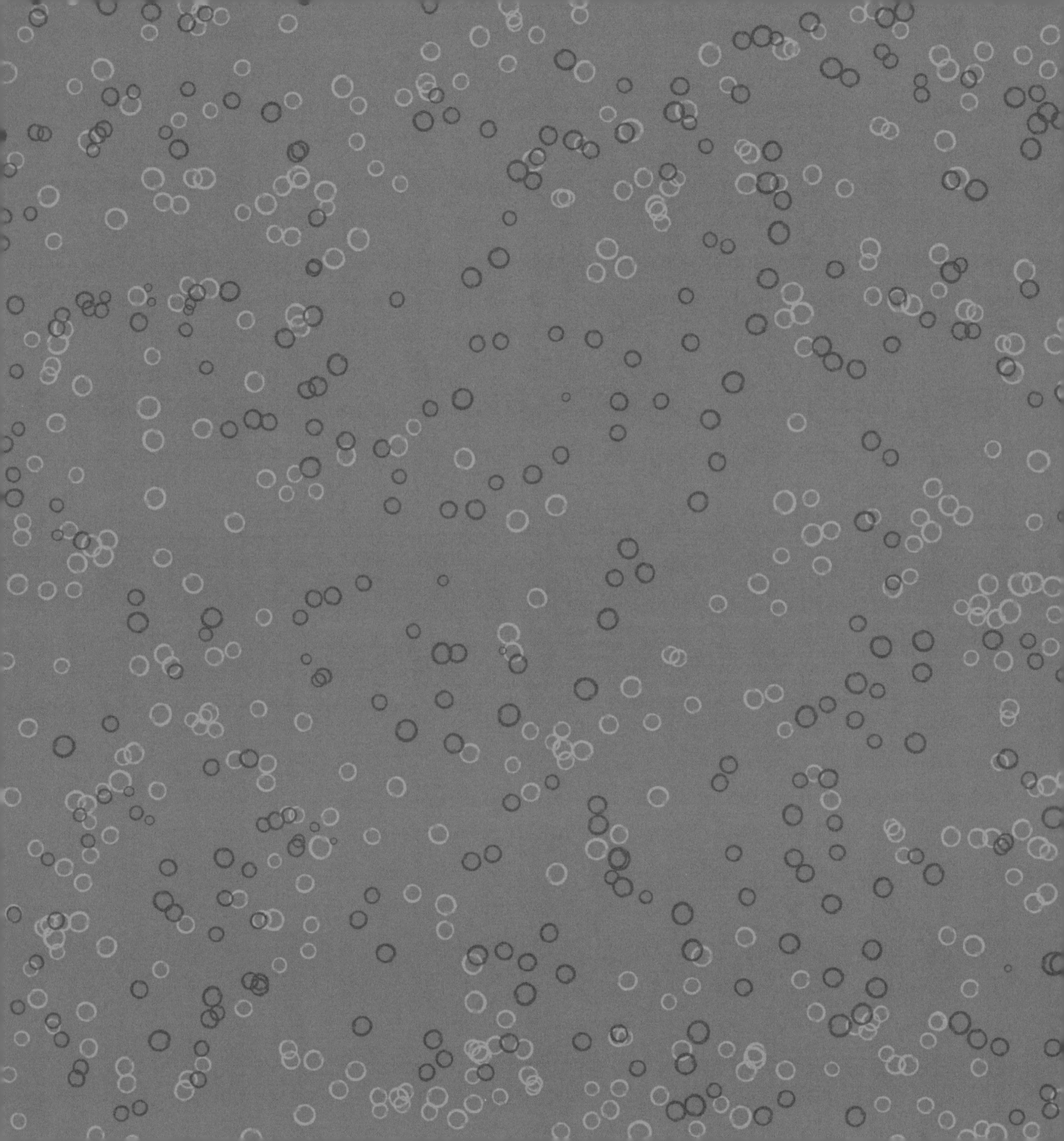

Soup Can Prank

Fool your family with this hilarious prank label!

1. Carefully cut out along the solid outline.
2. Wrap the label around the label of a real can of soup (or any can that fits) and tape to secure.
3. Put it back in the cupboard with the label facing out for your unsuspecting victim to discover!

cut the page from the book before you start making this project

Nutrition Facts

Serving Size	Total Fat 10g
1/2 cup (120ml)	Sat. Fat 5g
Servings about 2	Total Carb. 50g
	Fiber 1g
Calories 110	Sugars 30g
Fat Cal. 50	Cholest. 10mg
	Sodium 3000mg

Contains 150% RDA of 15 essential vitamins and minerals.

5143000 12434

Crampy's

CONDENSED

ALPHABET SNOT

NET WT.
10 OZ

SERVING SUGGESTION

QUICK AND EASY RECIPE

SNOTTY GREEN BEAN CASSEROLE

1 can Alphabet Snot
1 can Green Beans
2 sticks butter
1 can French Fried Onions (for garnish)

Mix all ingredients in large casserole (except onions). Bake in a 350° oven for 35 minutes or until bubbling. Garnish and serve immediately. Something spells delicious!

INGREDIENTS: SNOT, PHLEGM, MUCUS, BOOGERS, SALT, CORN OIL AND/OR PEANUT OIL AND/OR PALM KERNEL OIL, CORN SYRUP SOLIDS, FRUCTOSE, SUCROSE, SUGAR, ASPARTAME, SACCHARIN, NIACIN, FERROUS SULFATE, MODIFIED FOOD STARCH, SPICE EXTRACT, THIAMINE MONONITRATE, RIBOFLAVIN, FOLIC ACID, MONOSODIUM GLUTAMATE, ARTIFICIAL COLORING, FLAVOR.

PLEASE RECYCLE YOUR SNOT

STOP
Tip: Before gluing, fold the pieces into shape, then unfold and start gluing one tab at a time

Paper Crystals

Make these pretty gemstones to impress your friends.

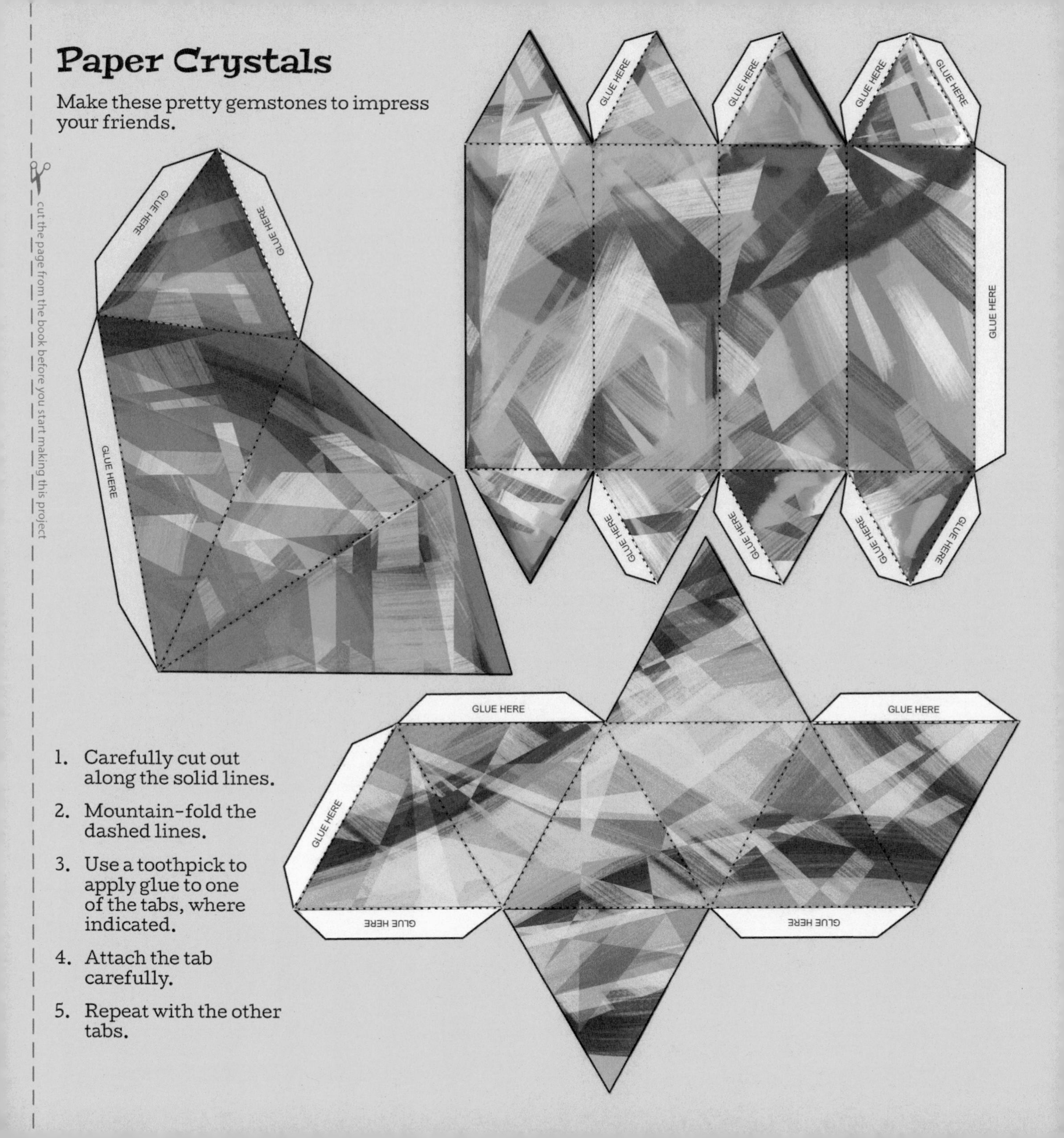

1. Carefully cut out along the solid lines.
2. Mountain-fold the dashed lines.
3. Use a toothpick to apply glue to one of the tabs, where indicated.
4. Attach the tab carefully.
5. Repeat with the other tabs.

Madcap Monster Maker

Make three cubes from the monstrous body parts on this page and the next page. Mix or match and stack the cubes to create the perfect creature. The combinations are practically endless!

1. Carefully cut out along the solid lines.
2. Mountain-fold along the dashed lines.
3. Fold into a cube, then unfold.
4. Use a toothpick to apply glue to one of the tabs, where indicated.
5. Attach the tab to the inside of the cube.
6. Repeat with the other tabs.

Tip: Before gluing, fold the pieces into shape, then unfold and start gluing one tab at a time

cut the page from the book before you start making this project

cut the page from the book before you start making this project

GLUE HERE

GLUE HERE

GLUE HERE

GLUE HERE

GLUE HERE

GLUE HERE

GLUE HERE

GLUE HERE

GLUE HERE

GLUE HERE

GLUE HERE

GLUE HERE

GLUE HERE

GLUE HERE

Pet Bugs

Make your very own pet bugs to name and play with!

1. Carefully cut out along the solid lines.
2. Fold along the dashed lines, making sure to use a Valley Fold or a Mountain Fold as indicated.

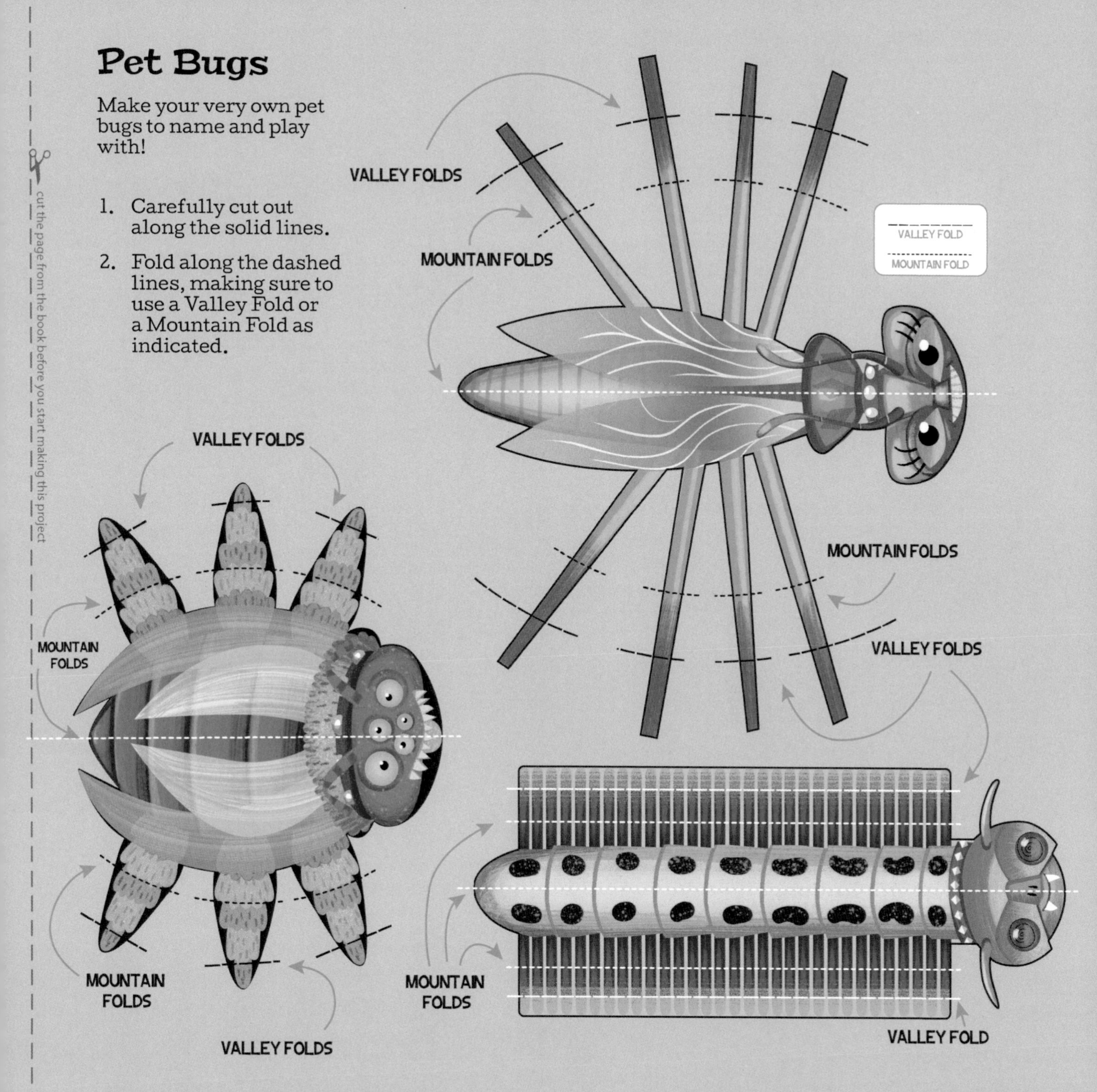

Tip: Go slow! Take your time cutting and folding

CAUTION! CAUTION!
ENTER AT
YOUR OWN
RISK!

Door Hanger

Assemble this Door Hanger and hang it outside your bedroom door.

1. Carefully cut out along the solid outline, then mountain-fold along the dashed lines.
2. Glue the two sides together and hang from your bedroom doorknob.

CLONING
COMPLETE
1
2

Clone Match Game

Play this fun matching card game with a friend.

1. Carefully cut along the solid lines of the cards on this page and the next page. You will have 30 cards total.
2. Shuffle the cards and arrange them in a grid, face-down on a tabletop.
3. Take turns, flipping over 2 cards per turn. If you get an exact match, keep the cards.
4. If your cards don't match exactly, replace the cards. Your turn is over.
5. When all the cards are gone, the player with the most cards wins!

cut the page from the book before you start making this project

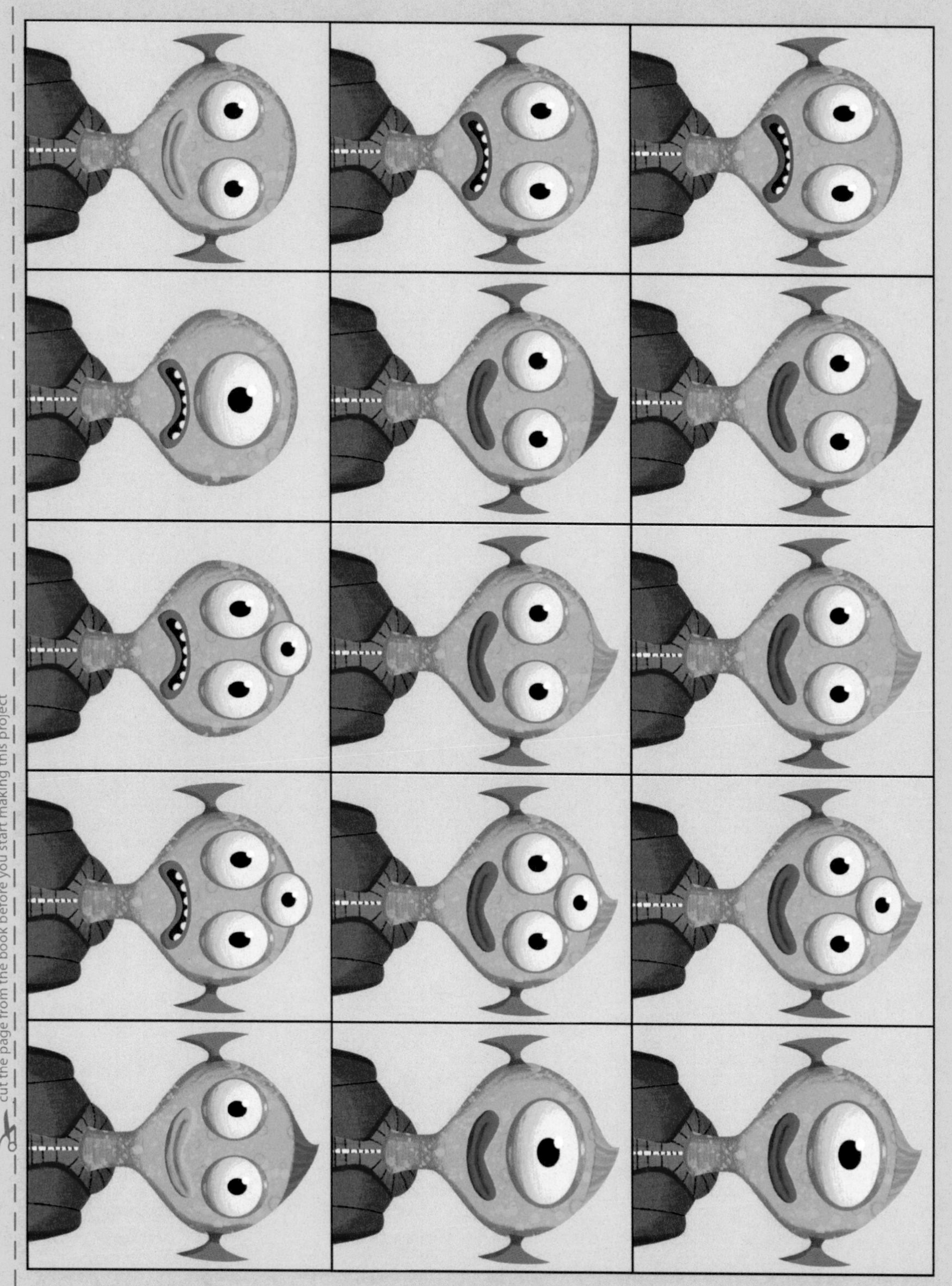

cut the page from the book before you start making this project

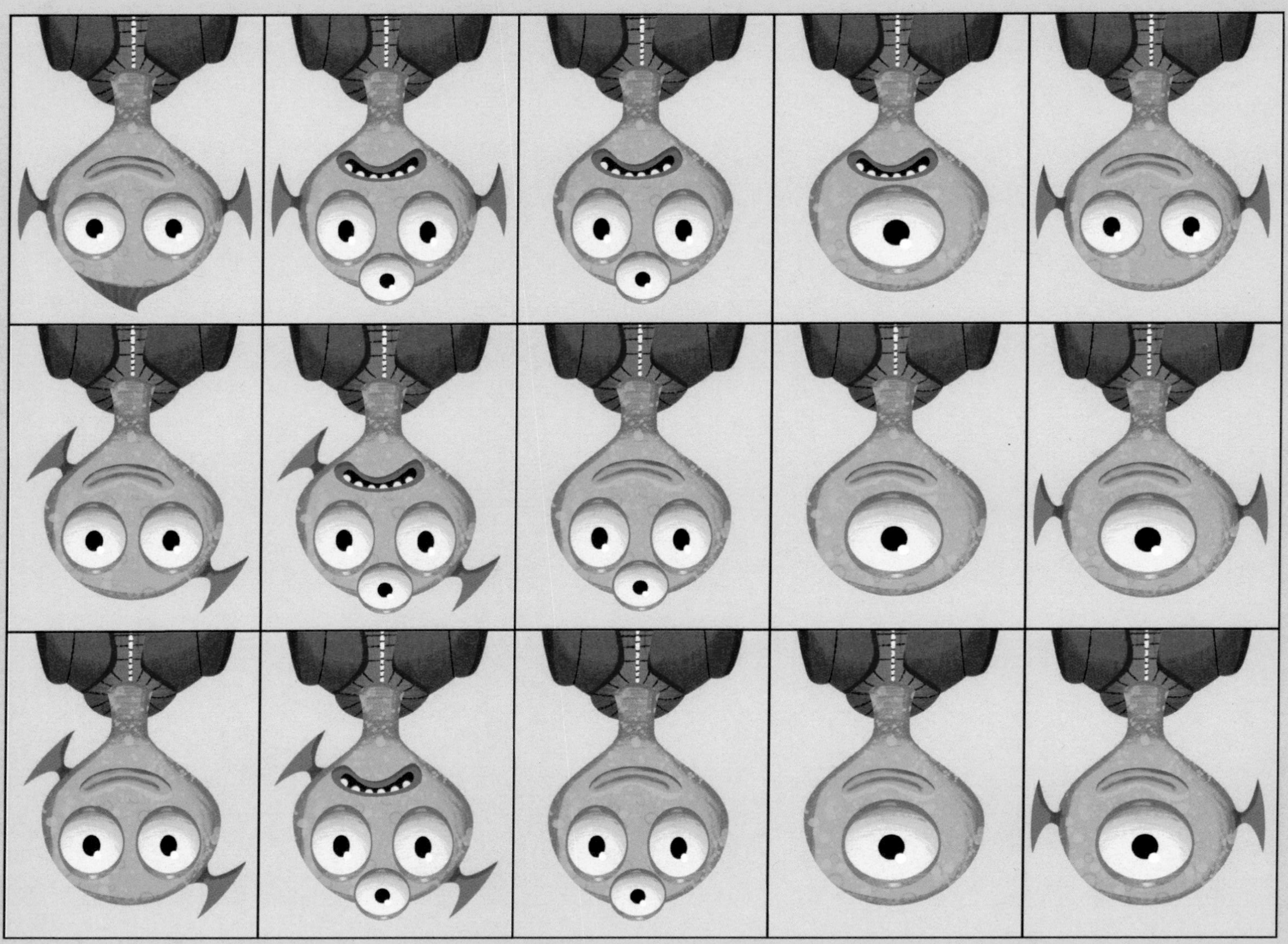

Grumpy Nesting Gnomes

This funny family of gnomes doesn't just live in the garden. They hide inside each other like nesting dolls!

1. Carefully cut out along the solid outlines.
2. Mountain-fold the tabs.
3. Twist the pieces so each gnome forms a cone.
4. Attach with glue or tape where indicated.

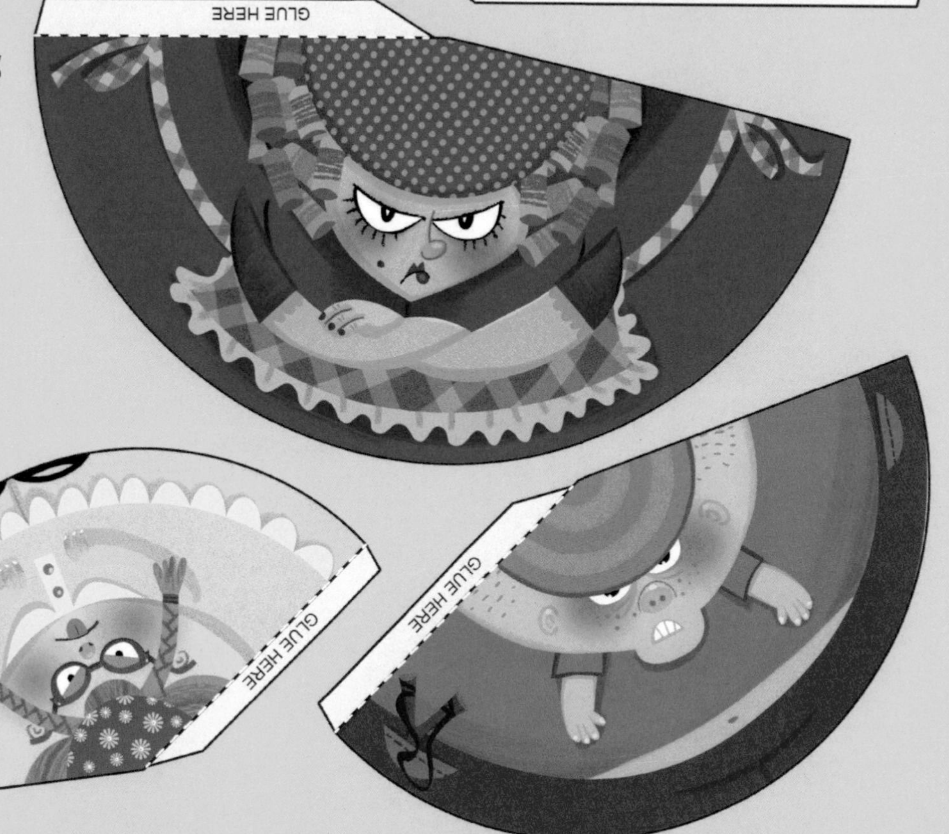

cut the page from the book before you start making this project

Ogre-Slayer Game

Play this fun game with a friend and see who can become the Ogre-Slayer first!

1. Carefully cut out the pawns and cards along the solid outlines.
2. Divide the pawns between 2 players. You will each have 8 pawns of the same color .
3. Take turns, placing 1 of your pawns onto the grid on the Ogre game board on the next page.
4. The first player to make any of the winning patterns with 4 of their pawns (see below) gets a Ruby card.
5. Start a new game.
6. The first player to collect 2 Ruby cards is the Ogre-Slayer!

WINNING PATTERNS

ACROSS

DOWN

DIAGONAL

SQUARE

cut the page from the book before you start making this project

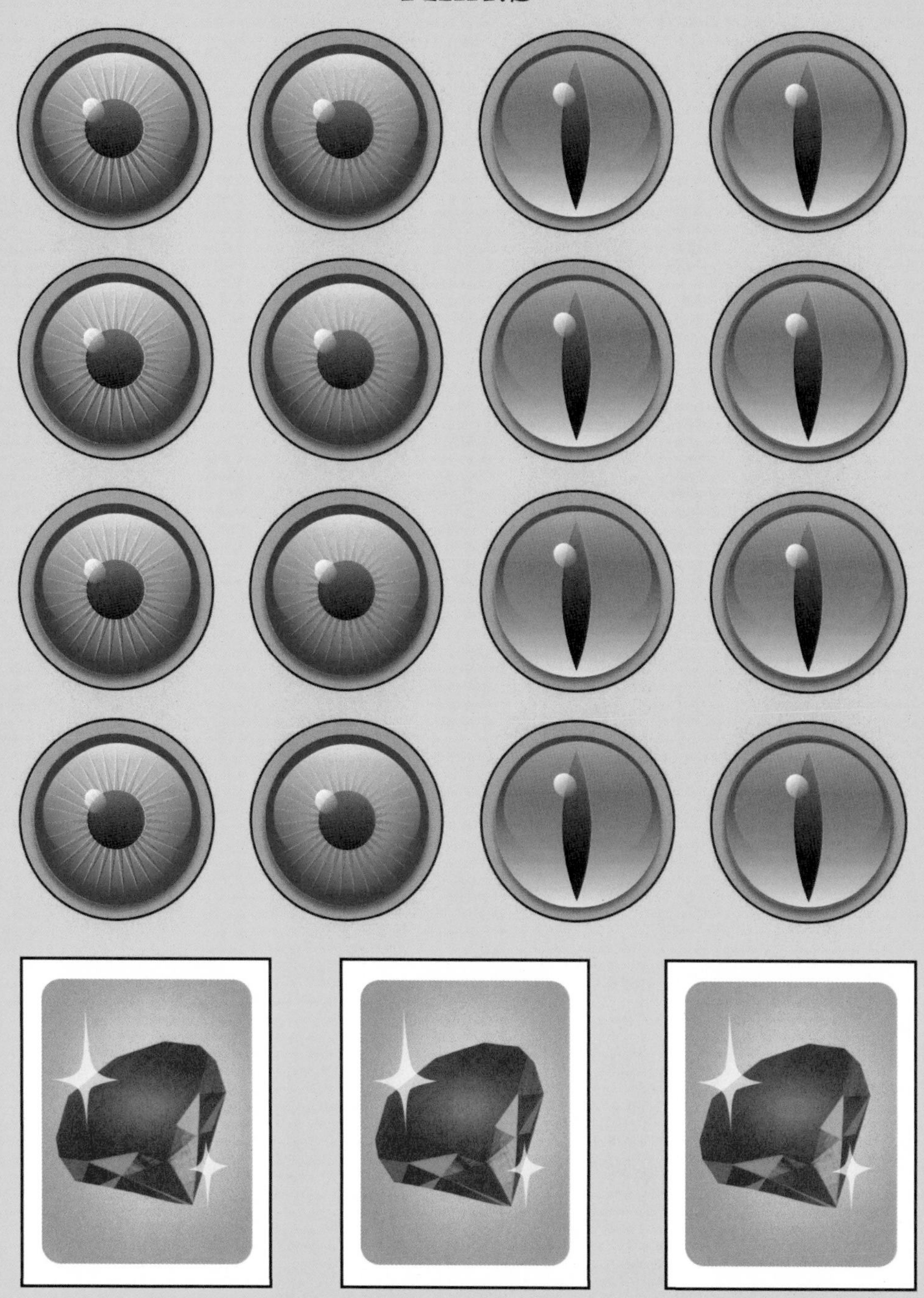

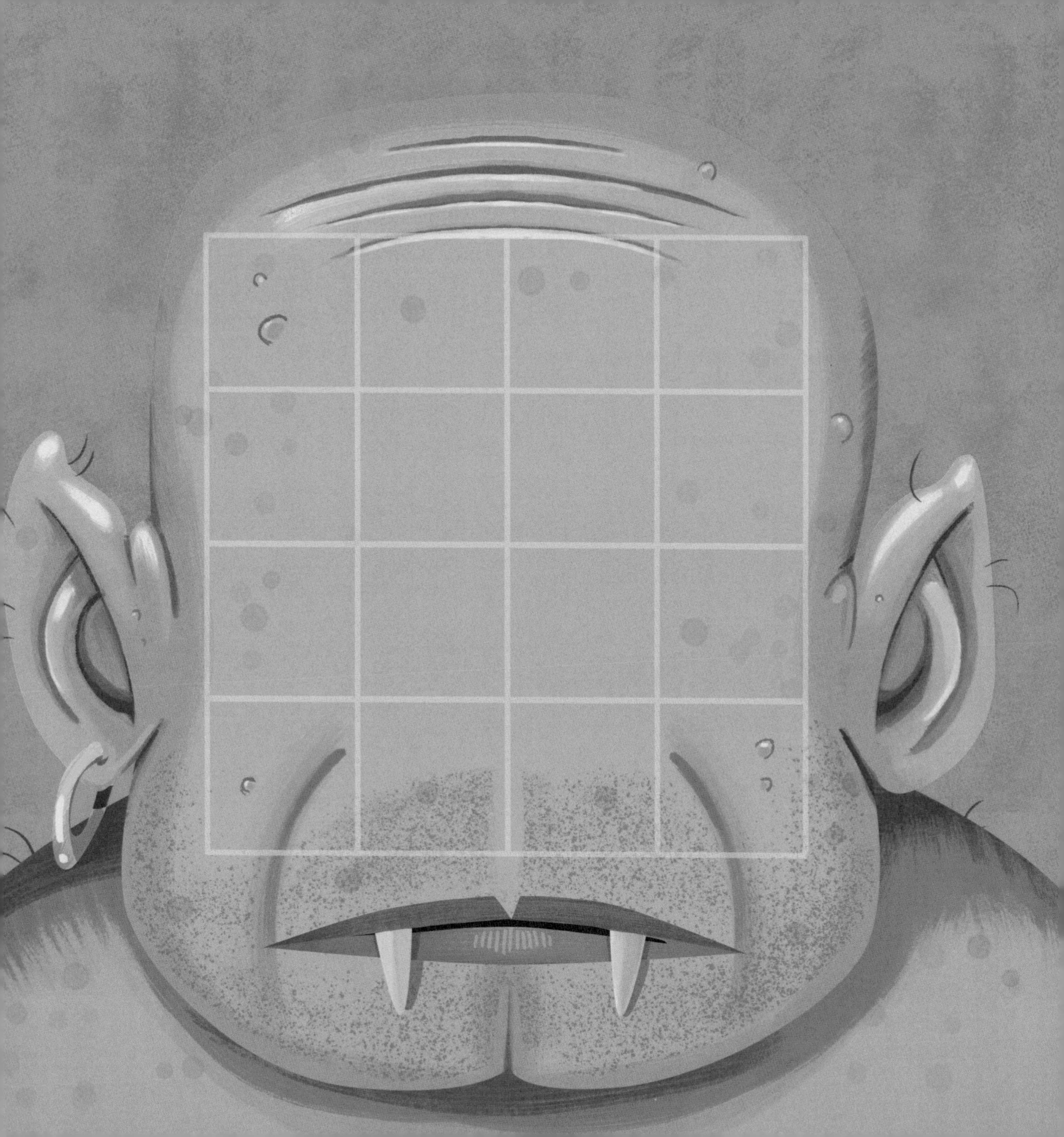

Misfortune Teller

Amaze your friends by revealing their doomed futures with this hilarious "cootie catcher" device.

1. Cut along the solid outline. Turn it face-down and position with a corner pointing down, as shown. Fold the top corner to the center.

2. Repeat with the other three corners. When you're done it will look like this.

3. Flip it over so the sides you just folded are face-down. Position it with a corner pointing down, as shown.

4. Fold the top corner to the center.

5. Repeat with the other three corners. When you're done it will look like this.

6. Fold it in half this way and unfold it.

7. Fold it in half the other way and unfold it.

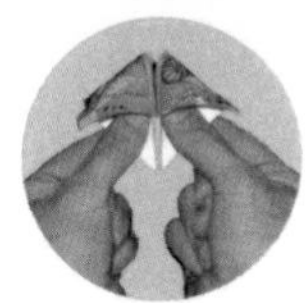

8. Slip your index fingers and thumbs inside the outer pockets and push them together to create the Teller.

How to use the device...

With the Misfortune Teller closed, ask your victim (um, your friend) to choose who they wish to reveal their fortune (Gypsy, Psychic, Swami or Chicken).

Now open-close-open the teller as shown below, spelling aloud their choice each time you open it.

With the teller open, ask them to choose a number shown inside. Open and close it again, counting aloud their choice each time you open it.

With it open, ask them to choose one of the fortune-telling methods shown inside the teller (Palmistry, for example). Lastly, peel back the panel they chose and read aloud the fortune directly beneath their choice.

  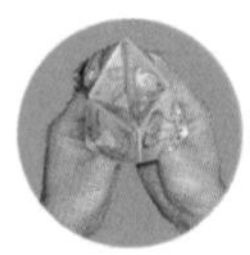  

S - W - A - M - I

cut the page from the book before you start making this project

Made in the USA
Middletown, DE
13 April 2020